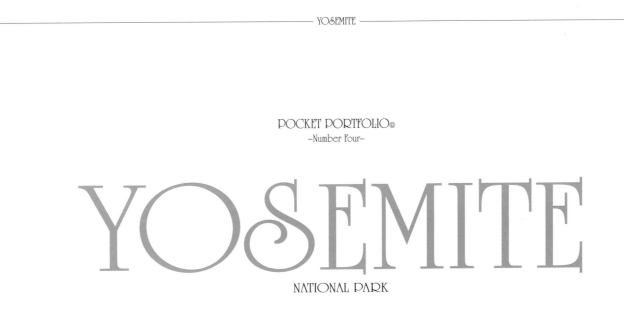

POCKET PORTFOLIO®
–Number Four–

YOSEMITE

NATIONAL PARK

including
LIVING IN YOSEMITE
by
LYNN WILSON

SIERRA PRESS
Mariposa, CA

ISBN 0-939365-58-8

PRODUCTION CREDITS

Book Design: Jeff Nicholas
Editor: Nicky Leach
Photo Editor: Jeff Nicholas
Captions: Jeff Nicholas
Printing coordination: Sung In Printing America, Inc.

PHOTO CREDITS

Carr Clifton: 30, 31
Ed Cooper: 2, 5
Chris Falkenstein (Falkfoto): 17, 25, 26
Michael Frye (Earthlight Photography): 12, 19, 32
Fred Hirschmann: 18 left
Richard Knepp: 15
William Neill: 29
Jeff Nicholas: 6, 13, 21, 27, 28
Galen Rowell (Mountain Light): 24 left, 10
Larry Ulrich: 16, 20, 24 right
Annette Bottaro-Walklet (Quietworks Photography): Front Cover, 16, Back Cover
Keith Walklet (Quietworks Photography): 7, 14, 22
Howard Weamer: 11, 18 right, 23
Jim Wilson: 1, 8, 9

Front Cover: Half Dome and rainbow, summer afternoon.
Frontispiece: Half Dome seen from Olmsted Point, sunset.
Title Page: Nevada Fall.
Back Cover: Apple tree in bloom and Upper Yosemite Fall.

The publishers would like to take this opportunity to
express our appreciation to the photographers who made
their imagery available for review during the editing of
this title. On behalf of those who will view this book—
Thank You!

If you would like to receive a complimentary
catalog of our publications,
please call: **(800) 745-2631**
e-mail: siepress@yosemite.net
or write: **SIERRA PRESS**
4988 Gold Leaf Drive, Mariposa, CA 95338

SIERRA PRESS

Yosemite Valley seen from Tunnel View, sunrise.

The grandeur of the scene was but softened by the haze that hung over the valley—light as gossamer—and by the clouds which partially dimmed the higher cliffs and mountains...as I looked, a peculiar exalted sensation seemed to fill my whole being, and I found my eyes in tears with emotion.

Lafayette Bunnell, 1851
Member, Mariposa Battalion

In 1851, Major James D. Savage and the 200 members of the Mariposa Battalion looked down into a valley in northern California that had been home to American Indians for more than 1,000 years. The Mariposa Battalion came upon the valley as they searched for a band of Southern Miwok people who called themselves the Ahwahneechee, after the Ahwahnee, or "deep grassy valley," in which they lived spring through fall. Within a year of the European discovery of the valley, the Ahwahneechee were forced out and their former homeland was renamed Yo-Semite, or "grizzly bear."

Ice and snow encrusted cliffs below Sentinel Rock.

After whites discovered Yosemite Valley in 1851, word spread quickly about its natural beauty. Heavy use started to have a negative effect on the plants and animals that lived in the valley. In 1864, public concern led California Senator John Conness to introduce a bill calling for protection of the lands. Quickly passed by Congress and signed by President Abraham Lincoln, this historic legislation made a land grant to the state of California consisting of both Yosemite Valley and the Mariposa Grove of Big Trees, protecting and holding them "inalienable for all time." The Yosemite Land Grant set a precedent that, in 1872, paved the way for America's first national park—Yellowstone. In 1890, 2 million acres of lands surrounding Yosemite Valley and Mariposa Grove were set aside for federal protection as Yosemite National Park—America's third national park. The original Yosemite Land Grant was later incorporated into the national park.

I LIVE, WORK, AND PLAY IN YOSEMITE NATIONAL PARK. Through the years I've watched shadows lengthen on pine trees and widen on stately oaks. I observe where last winter's fallen limbs have left jagged amputation scars, and I mourn the uprooting of a familiar evergreen. I feel a relationship with each tree, each rock, and each flower I pass on my 5 A.M. drive to work. As the seasons unfold, my excitement grows, for there are always new and exciting events in this natural world.

Nature, here, is the master architect, and she is relentless in redefining her landscape. She fingers her way into the heart of rocks, sends down massive slides, and transforms, yet again, her stony facades. She blows hot breath and causes wildfires to ignite, destroying plants, animals, and the works of man. Yet, that same destruction replenishes the earth with vital minerals and nutrients, and, like the phoenix, a future forest arises from the ashes of the past. Ground-shaking, loam-rolling earthquakes shake out unstable rocks and toss them effortlessly aside. And great floods, like the One Hundred Year Flood of 1997, scour away the old and reveal the new. I've seen Yosemite change a great deal in my time here, and there is only one thing I know to be true: the free spirit of nature cannot be controlled, for she alone knows how to reevaluate, reorganize, and rebuild.

How I love October. The days shorten, the nights lengthen, and the sounds of autumn flutter on the brisk breeze. Migrating birds cast moving shadows across the land. Fresh summer green is replaced with a kaleidoscope of warm autumnal hues. I treasure the sound of whirling leaves as they scratch the soil. The wind dies, slowly raining its captive foliage to the earth. I watch squirrels urgently bury another cheekful of gathered nuts, leaving their pine cone litter to blend with the now needle-carpeted forest floor. Gentle showers wash the air of dust, leaving the fresh scent of negatively charged ions to perfume the air. The river, now slowed to a trickle, swirls another booty of multicolored leaves. During these days, my morning commute is usually silent, broken only by an occasional coyote howl or the prehistoric call of a great blue heron.

Opposite: Half Dome and Yosemite backcountry seen from Sentinel Dome, sunset.

Hillside of California poppies, Merced river Canyon.

Yosemite's broad range of elevations, exposures, precipitation levels, and soil conditions attract more than 1,400 types of trees, shrubs, and wildflowers to grow in the park. On the park's west side, oak- and pine-clad foothills sizzle in March with orange hordes of California poppies. Higher up, Wawona and Yosemite Valley support evergreen Douglas fir, incense cedar, and, in some locations, giant sequoia interspersed with deciduous big-leaf maple, Pacific dogwood, and black oak. Between Chinquapin and Glacier Point, or Crane Flat and Tuolumne Meadows, mild wet winters and warm summers nourish dense forests of lodgepole pine, red fir, ponderosa pine, and sugar pine, and meadow dwellers such as lupine, bistort, and camas lily, which thrive in clearings. Spring reaches the High Sierra in July and August. In Tuolumne Meadows, snowmelt and warmer temperatures awaken wildflowers surrounded by lodgepole, hemlock, and aspen, while up on Yosemite's granite rooftop, miniature lupine, penstemon, and daisy form colorful alpine mats beside *krummholz* trees that have been tortured and twisted by extreme weather, yet still survive.

Winter creeps in, filling my home with an odor-less purity—clean, silent, and peaceful. Cotton-ball snow-puffs soften the curves of the landscape. Winter's white blanket drapes the black limbs of oaks, and icicles hang from evergreen branches. Snow-flocked trees, resting on massif brows, create a stark contrast with the lapis sky. Cliffs reflect lunar light and reveal sleeping shadows of days gone by and glaciers yet unborn. I glide atop tomorrow's meadow on my skis and bask in the pale light of the solstice moon.

In late March, warmer air begins to chase away winter's last chill. Far beneath the surface of the land, un-seen, unfelt, the earth stirs. I smell the first fragrance of fertility as it rises from the boggy meadows. Half Dome looms in silhouetted silence, bowing gracefully to the blue-violet birth of day. Wildland babes take their first breath of life, and the music of black-headed grosbeaks announces the arrival of spring.

April showers wash the earth with gentle spring rain. Standing on Pohono Bridge, I can see bare-branched dogwoods dappled with creamy white bracts that appear to float in mid-air. I drive beneath the delicate lime-green tassels that dangle from the maples overhanging the road, and I am inspired by soft mats of purple lupine coloring the causeways between ancient conifers. As the weather grows balmier, vernal runoff surges exuberantly from gran-

Bracken fern and Douglas fir cone, Yosemite Valley.

ite precipices, quenching the Merced River's thirst with the season's first taste of melted snow. Soon, the snow will be gone, and dry days of summer will slow the river to a mere shadow of its springtime self.

During spring run-off, I usually take an evening walk to Yosemite Falls. Swirling spray at the base of the falls couples with light from the full moon and a ghostly lunar rainbow appears. Mist-drenched, I watch from the bridge as the moonbows dance to the pulse of surging water. In two more weeks, when the moon has gone, I'll walk to Chapel Meadow. I will align myself perfectly, so that the North Star lies cradled in the granite groove at the top of Yosemite Falls. With myriad stars as my companions, summer dreams are close at hand.

El Capitan and Yosemite Valley from Valley View, winter sunset.

The towering cliffs of Yosemite Valley were created by the Merced Glacier. The glacier reached its maximum size about 1 million years ago, when it extended as far west as El Portal and buried the valley to within 700 feet of the summit of Half Dome. Following the V-shaped canyon already created by the Merced River, it extended as far west as El Portal. By 250,000 years ago the glacier had retreated, leaving behind a deeply quarried, U-shaped valley. The last glacier to affect Yosemite, about 30,000 years ago, had a lasting effect on the floor of the valley. When it retreated it left behind a huge berm of eroded material at its point of maximum advance, known as a terminal moraine (between El Capitan and Bridalveil Fall.) The moraine created a lake that inundated the valley. Over millennia, Lake Yosemite gradually filled with more than 2,000 feet of sediments washed down from the high country, then disappeared. The flat floor of today's Yosemite Valley is really a lake bed.

Bigelow sneezeweed in Cooks Meadow, Yosemite Valley.

Young saw-whet owl in its nest.

Dogwood blossoms and the Merced River, spring.

The rich floral diversity found in the Yosemite region provides for the needs of an astonishing array of animal life. Although plants are fairly restricted to particular communities and elevations, animals—especially birds and larger mammals—tend to roam from area to area and migrate seasonally. More than 80 mammal species occupy Yosemite. Visitors to the park may expect to see mule deer and coyotes, among others. More rarely encountered are black bear, bighorn sheep, and mountain lions. In addition to these larger mammals are dozens of less conspicuous residents— chickarees, marmots, pikas, and foxes—to name a few. Sharing the resources with the mammals are many fish, amphibian, and reptile species. More than 230 species of birds have also been identified, from golden eagles and peregrine falcons to kingfishers, water ouzels, and Stellers jays, which seem to visit every picnic table in the park.

Bridalveil Fall and Yosemite Valley seen from Tunnel View, summer afternoon.

Prior to the onset of glaciation, some 3 million years ago, Yosemite Valley was a V-shaped, river-cut canyon, nearly 3,000 feet deep. Tributary streams, such as Bridalveil and Yosemite Creeks, were unable to cut as deeply as the Merced River because of their smaller size. Instead, they tumbled down the sloping canyon walls in a series of cascades and small falls. Following glaciation, 1 million years ago, the V-shaped canyon had been deepened and widened, creating the U-shape seen today. Tributaries, and their valleys, were left under-cut and suspended high above the new valley floor as "hanging valleys." In the eastern end of the valley, Yosemite Falls plummets more than 2,400 feet in three dramatic stages—Upper Fall free-falls 1,430 feet before striking the mid-section. In the valley's western end, Bridalveil Fall twists and turns during its 620-foot descent, often buffeted by the winds common in this end of the valley.

Upper Yosemite Fall and "normal" spring flooding in Cooks Meadow.

IN MID-AUGUST, I ASSEMBLE A PICNIC dinner and make my way to Sentinel Dome to view the annual Perseid meteor shower. I hear the distant echo of Vernal and Nevada Falls as I watch the last embers of the day tint the face of Half Dome. I lean on the solitary corpse of the much-photographed lone Jeffery pine and feel the day's remaining warmth enter me. This tree, this place, this solitude—is utter. I find a cozy rock and face the southern sky as the meteor shower blazes across the midnight sky, burst upon burst. I sacrifice my sleep willingly for this chance to witness the trails stars walk.

On another day, my husband and I pack a knapsack and head for the Mariposa Grove of Big Trees. On our honeymoon, Jim and I marked our union by having a picture taken of us driving through the Wawona Tree. We were one of the last to drive through this giant before it fell that winter. Wawona is an Indian word describing the hooting of owls. Jim and I rest against the Wawona Tree's thick bark, lovingly reminisce, and listen for an occasional hoot.

We commune with "our" tree, then walk on to the Grizzly Giant. Standing beneath its massive branches (bigger than most tree trunks), I am aware of how small human beings really are. I feel humbled, for this noble giant has been battered by centuries of fire, lightning, and snow, yet it wears its scars with the pride of a survivor. I pause for a moment and allow the tree to become my teacher. I see how I'm drawn to "damaged" trees, to their uniqueness and beauty. Their weathered spirit never gives up the fight, and their battle marks only distinguish them further. I think about how human beings treat their own "battle-scarred" populations. With honor or contempt? A perplexing question.

The Grizzly Giant, Mariposa Grove, winter.

In 1857, Galen Clark was the first European to enter the forest of sequoias that he named Mariposa Grove. Sequoias were officially recognized by scientists in 1852, but their enormous size was generally considered a hoax. To persuade the public of the sequoias' size, the state of California allowed the cutting of entire trees, which were then shipped in sections to the East Coast. A 20-foot cross-section was even sent to the United States Centennial Exposition in 1875. The giant sequoia (*Sequoiadendron giganteum*) is a relict species, left over from cooler times, and may be 150 million years old. It has only two known relatives: California's coastal redwood (*Sequoia sempervirens*) and the dawn redwood (*Metasequoia*), which is found only in China.

Dogwood tree in autumnal color phase, Yosemite Valley.

Lower Chilnualna Fall, Wawona area.

Historic covered bridge and South Fork of the Merced River, Wawona.

The same elevation as Yosemite Valley (4,000 feet), Wawona was first settled by non-Indians when Galen Clark built Clark's Station in 1857. The lush, sunny meadows bordering the South Fork of the Merced River became a popular stopover for sightseers visiting the newly discovered Mariposa Grove of Big Trees nearby, en route to Yosemite Valley. A major proponent of protection for the Big Trees, Clark became the first guardian of Yosemite Valley and the Mariposa Grove of Big Trees when they were set aside as the Yosemite Land Grant in 1864. In 1874, Clark sold his "station" to the Washburn brothers, who changed its name to Big Tree Station. In 1882, one of the brothers suggested the name of Wawona for the adjoining village, a name the local Southern Miwok people had given to the Big Trees. Thought by whites to mean "big trees", Wawona was actually a Miwok word that imitated the hoot of an owl, a creature considered by the Miwok to be the guardian spirit/deity of the giant sequoia forest.

Krummholz Jeffrey pine (misshapen by severe conditions) atop Sentinel Dome, sunset.

Exposed roots of a toppled giant sequoia, Upper Mariposa Grove.

Fire scarred sequoia trunks, Mariposa Grove.

The western slope of California's Sierra Nevada, between 5,000 and 7,000 feet in elevation, is the only place on the planet where giant sequoias grow naturally. Within this area—260 miles long and 30 miles wide—are found 75 small groves of the most massive life-form ever to have evolved on earth. Old-growth trees sprout from seeds so small it requires 91,000 of them to make up a pound. They average 10 to 15 feet in diameter but can exceed 30 feet and, although they are not the tallest trees on earth (California's coastal redwoods are), some sequoias are known to have attained heights in excess of 300 feet. In addition to its great size, the sequoia is also long-lived. The oldest authenticated age for a giant sequoia is 3,200 years. The largest sequoia in Yosemite, the Grizzly Giant found in Mariposa Grove, is estimated to be more than 2,700 years of age. The name sequoia was first used by scientists in 1852 and was given in honor of Sequoyah, chief of the Cherokee Nation, who, in 1821, created an alphabet for his people.

Mount Starr King and high-country domes, winter.

DURING SUMMER MONTHS I dedicate my free time to the high country, my favorite place to relax and explore. I love the subalpine meadows, with their carpets of soft green grass and rainbows of wildflowers. They are so fragile and their growing season so short, they must spend each day ensuring their survival. In order to compete for sun, space, and insect pollinators, these little flowers produce large vibrant blossoms.

The meadows are so aromatic, they beckon me to strap on my backpack and head for the high country. Not far along the trail, I come to Twin Bridges, which spans the Lyell Fork of the Tuolumne River. I stop to rest on the bridge and watch the meandering current. Snowmelt produces unparalleled clarity. Pebbles, some large, some red, some crystalloid with feldspar, melodically tumble in the babbling course. Looking upstream, I can make out every boulder, every piece of wood, and every clump of moss as far as the eye can see. My mind absorbs this clarity and looks back at the earth with a different eye.

I stop at a signed trail junction. A right turn leads to Vogelsang High Sierra Camp. Straight ahead, about 200 miles on the John Muir Trail, is Mount Whitney. I spent three months hiking the John Muir trail many years ago. It is a land of water—transparent lakes, ice-blue glaciers, coursing rivers, and jack-knife waterfalls. The memories make me sigh momentarily, then I make a right turn and head for Vogelsang Peak.

One million years ago, nearly all of Yosemite lay buried beneath two massive glaciers—the Tuolumne and the Merced Glaciers. Both followed paths already established by rivers of the same names. The 60-mile-long Tuolumne Glacier, the largest ever to form in the Sierra Nevada, carved the spectacular Grand Canyon of the Tuolumne and the Hetch Hetchy Valley—Yosemite's northern "twin." The Merced Glacier carved Little Yosemite Valley and then, after being joined by an arm of the Tuolumne Glacier at the base of Half Dome, proceeded to carve Yosemite Valley. In 1871, the famous conservationist John Muir discovered the remnants of Merced Glacier. It strengthened his bold new theory about the glacial origins of Yosemite Valley. The accepted theory at the time was that a cataclysmic event, such as an earthquake, had formed the valley. The Merced Glacier melted in 1977, but three others survive in the park—The Dana, Conness, and Lyell Glaciers, found on the peaks of the same names.

Opposite: Alpine tarn and glaciated ridge, Yosemite high-country.

Hanging meadow on the slopes of Mount Conness.   Late summer color on shore of Siesta Lake (7,500 feet elevation).

Spanish explorers, who saw this great mountain range from afar in 1772, named it *una gran sierra nevada*—
"a great snow-covered range." Paralleling the eastern border of California for 400 miles, it is the longest
unbroken mountain range in the United States. Its great length and height—it rises nearly three miles above the
Central Valley—form an enormous natural barrier for warm, moisture-laden storms sweeping in from the Pacific.
Forced upward by the barrier, incoming storm clouds are slowed and cooled, causing the moisture they carry to
grow heavy enough to fall as rain or, if swept upward into even colder air, as snow. In Yosemite, the greatest
precipitation falls between 5,000 and 9,000 feet. Mariposa Grove (6,000 feet) averages more than 45 inches of
precipitation (mostly winter snow) annually. Interestingly, both the town of Mariposa (2,000 feet) and Tioga Pass
(9,941 feet) average the same annual precipitation—30 inches. The difference is that rain falls on Mariposa while
the equivalent of 30 inches of rain falls, as snow, in the high country.

The trail steeply switchbacks through lodgepole pines. At my feet is purple larkspur, whose fragrant blossoms whirl around a single stem, shriveled with age at the bottom yet budding at the tip. Crimson columbines lace the trail, their flaming red flowers and zesty yellow throats floating in a sea of forest green. I stop to inhale their sweet aroma. Bright-red Indian paintbrush polka-dot the spaces between the lodgepole pines. I hear a trickle of water. Orange- and maroon-speckled leopard lilies divulge the location of Rafferty Creek. I am caught in the warmth of the day, the heady scent of the forest, and the dazzling colors of woodland flowers. I reach the top of the trail before I know it.

Half Dome and clearing winter storm seen from Glacier Point.

I descend from the brow of Lyell Canyon into a gently sloping meadow with a network of tunnels crisscrossing its lavish green surface. A high-pitched chirp breaks the silence. I look around to see what is making the alarm call. Sitting perched on its hind legs is a fat and furry Belding ground squirrel warning others of my presence. Out of the corner of my eye, I see a number of young squirrels scurry into a hole and peek out. Perhaps they think I can't see them. I chuckle silently and continue my hike. This long luxuriant meadow draws to a close, and I start to climb the last steep leg to camp.

I pitch my tent, hang my food, and gently release my sore feet from tight hiking boots. I playfully run through the soft alpine grass, then swoosh the waters of Upper Fletcher Lake between my toes. Ah!! The cool liquid comforts my swollen feet. Leaning back on my hands, I notice the sharp contrast between the stark granite peaks and the lush meadow. The pure air envelops me. The blue sky seems to press against my body. My noise-battered ears listen intently for a single sound in this absolute silence.

Tuolumne River, winter in Tuolumne Meadows.

Behind me, a playful marmot skitters across the scree. I turn quickly and catch a glimpse of him sneaking between the boulders. He zigs and zags, dodging periodically out of sight as if he is playing hide and seek with me. As he gets nearer, he stops, crouches behind a giant rock, and peers out at me. I'm not sure who is more curious, the marmot or me. After this tentative introduction he seems reassured, leaps onto a boulder, and proceeds to entertain me. I soon forget how tired I am and my inner child starts to laugh and clap her hands. This inspires the marmot even more and he becomes quite the ham. The light fades and the marmot leaves. Alpine glow from Fletcher Peak casts a golden reflection on the waters of the lake. Later, in my tent, I quickly fall asleep, dreaming of marmots, Beldings, and carpets of alpine wildflowers.

My travels must soon come to an end, so I am up at dawn retracing the path back to Tuolumne Meadows and my car. I stop for lunch by a small, crystal-clear waterfall that runs freely between soft green grass and hard, gray stone. Suddenly, an ear-piercing shriek breaks the midday tranquility. I catch sight of a golden eagle soaring on the updrafts above Rafferty Creek's turfy margins. My eyes fixed, arm hairs standing straight up, I watch him glide the thermals. As I leave, I keep gazing into the heavens for another glimpse of the eagle, then I realize he is accompanying me down the path. We play tag for nearly two hours. I am so engrossed watching him, I nearly trip over my own feet. He is my last companion on the trail home. As I open the car door, I look up one last time and watch him soar away. Goodbye, good friend.

After all these years in Yosemite, I realize it's not just the eternal gray of granite that drains age from me nor just the salve of alpine light that rejuvenates my soul. It is the solitude, the expanses of time and space, and my backyard companions that keep me young. Memories, like meteors dashing across midnight skies, arrive, sparkle, and vanish. . .but not forever. Somewhere, deep within me, stars, lakes, flowers, and granite leave their indelible trail.

Summer sunset in Tuolumne Meadows.

Tuolumne Meadows, the largest subalpine meadow in the Sierra Nevada, lay buried beneath glacial ice until the end of the last ice age, 10,000 years ago. As temperatures warmed, the glacier retreated and melted. This meltwater collected in depressions scoured and polished by the glacier, forming cold, clear, lifeless ponds, pools, and lakes. Gradually sediments were washed into standing water, where they accumulated and provided a foothold for sedges and willows at the water's edge. Some pools collected enough sediments and decomposing plants from early colonizers that they became marshlike, allowing grasses and water-loving trees to grow. As the water table lowered a meadow formed. Eventually, if the water table continues lower, trees, such as aspens, followed by conifers, will take over. Tuolumne Meadows has already undergone the complete pool-to-forest transformation once. A dense forest of lodgepole pine developed here prior to the Little Ice Age, 2,500 years ago. As temperatures cooled the water table was raised, drowning the roots of the forest, recreating the meadows. If the water table lowers again, the forest of lodgepole pine will gradually return.

Glaciated shoreline of Tenaya Lake, summer afternoon.

The granite from which the Sierra Nevada has been sculpted formed 85 to 130 million years ago as a batholith, or "stone of the depths." During a period of volcanism a great body of magma (molten earth) cooled and hardened beneath the surface of the earth. It lay beneath older volcanic peaks as high as 13,000 feet, which had reached the surface as lava. By 65 million years ago, most of these mountains had been removed by erosion and the underlying batholith was exposed. Over the next 40 million years the granite was eroded into low hills and broad valleys, through which the ancestral Merced and Tuolumne Rivers meandered. About 10 million years ago, the entire region began to be uplifted and tilted to the west causing the rivers to accelerate and downcut their channels. Prior to the onset of glaciation, 3 million years ago, the Sierra had been uplifted to near its present height and both rivers had incised V-shaped valleys—some as deep as 3,000 feet—into the granite bedrock.

Glacial polish near Olmsted Point, sunset.

Melting snow in Dana Meadow below Mammoth Peak, early summer.

The monolithic appearance of the Sierra Nevada, which John Muir eloquently named "the Range of Light," is deceptive. The granite is riven with cracks, fractures, and faults. Some of these were created when the magma that formed the granite cooled and hardened; others formed when the granite expanded as the weight of overlying materials was removed by erosion; and still others are the result of the ongoing uplifting and tilting that continues to shape California. For the past 50 million years these weak areas have provided paths of least resistance for the agents of erosion: wind, water, snow, and ice. By a million years ago, glaciers had not only filled, deepened, and widened the river canyons but covered most of the Yosemite region, sculpting and polishing the landscape as they pursued their downhill courses. Today—following the retreat of the glaciers— water once again flows along those same paths of least resistance taken by the ancestral rivers.

Opposite: Waterwheel Falls, Grand Canyon of the Tuolumne River.

FOR MORE INFORMATION

YOSEMITE NATIONAL PARK
P.O. Box 577
Yosemite, Ca 95389
(209) 372-0200, TDD (209) 372-4726
www.nps.gov/yose/

**VISIT THE NATIONAL PARKS ON
THE INTERNET:** www.nps.gov

YOSEMITE ASSOCIATION
P.O. Box 230
El Portal, Ca 95318
www.yosemite.org

ACCOMMODATIONS

LODGING INSIDE THE PARK:
Yosemite Concession Services
(209) 252-4848
www.yosemitepark.com

CAMPING INSIDE THE PARK:
Yosemite Concession Services
(800) 436-PARK, TDD (888) 530-9796,
International (301) 722-1257
www.yosemitepark.com

LODGING OUTSIDE THE PARK:
Mammoth Visitor Center
Mammoth Lakes, CA 93546
(760) 924-5500
www.r5.fs.fed.us/inyo

Mariposa County Visitors Bureau
Mariposa, CA 95338
(888) 554-9012
www.mariposa.org

Tuolumne County Visitors Bureau
Sonora, Ca 95370
(800) 446-1333
www.thegreatunfenced.com

Yosemite Sierra Visitors Bureau
Oakhurst, CA 93644
(559) 683-4636
www.yosemite-sierra.org

★Portland

★Reno

★San Francisco

★YOSEMITE

★Las Vegas

★Los Angeles

★Phoenix

Photo: Mule deer buck, Yosemite Valley.